The Nature Kid's Guide to
TARANTULAS

DAVID ANDERSON

LP Media Inc. Publishing
Text copyright © 2026 by LP Media Inc.

For information address LP Media Inc. Publishing,
30012 Variolite St NW, Princeton MN 55371
www.lpmedia.org

Publication Data

Tarantulas
The Nature Kid's Guide to Tarantulas — First edition.

Summary: "Learn all about Tarantulas, the Nature Kid Way"
— Provided by publisher.

ISBN: 979-8-89818-221-2

[1. Tarantulas – Non-Fiction] I. Title.

Title: The Nature Kid's Guide to Tarantulas

CONTENTS

DARK DENS

Some tarantulas don't dig their own holes — they move into burrows already dug by mice or lizards!

Scritch, scritch! A Mexican Red Knee tarantula digs a cozy burrow in the dirt.

Tarantulas are big, hairy spiders. They live in warm places all over the world. You can find them in deserts, forests, and grassy hills.

Many tarantulas dig burrows in the ground. A burrow is like a small tunnel that can reach 2 feet deep. The spider lines it with soft silk and waits inside for prey to pass by.

The Mexican Red Knee makes its home in rocky slopes. It stays in the shade during the hot day. At sundown, it creeps out to find food.

WORLD WIDE
FUN FACT!
Tarantulas have been on Earth for more than 100 million years — they lived alongside dinosaurs!

Rustle! A King Baboon tarantula crawls through dry grass on an African plain.

Tarantulas live all over the world. They are found on six of seven continents. Only icy Antarctica has none.

Many kinds live in South America. Others live in Africa, Asia, and the United States. Some even live on warm islands in the Pacific Ocean.

The King Baboon lives in East Africa. It likes hot, open grasslands where the soil is hard and dry. This spider digs deep burrows to stay cool during the blazing afternoon heat.

SIZE UP

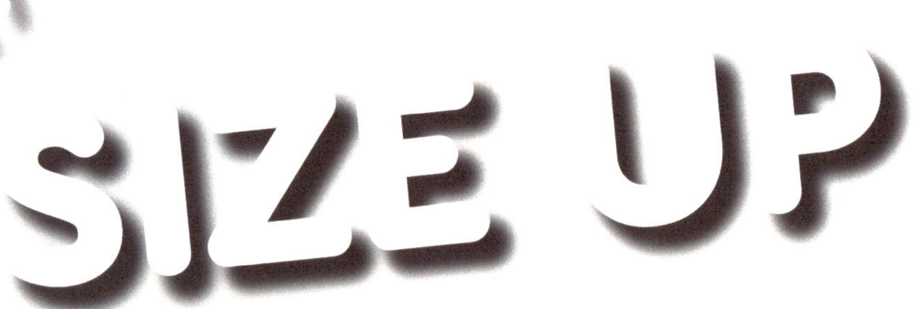

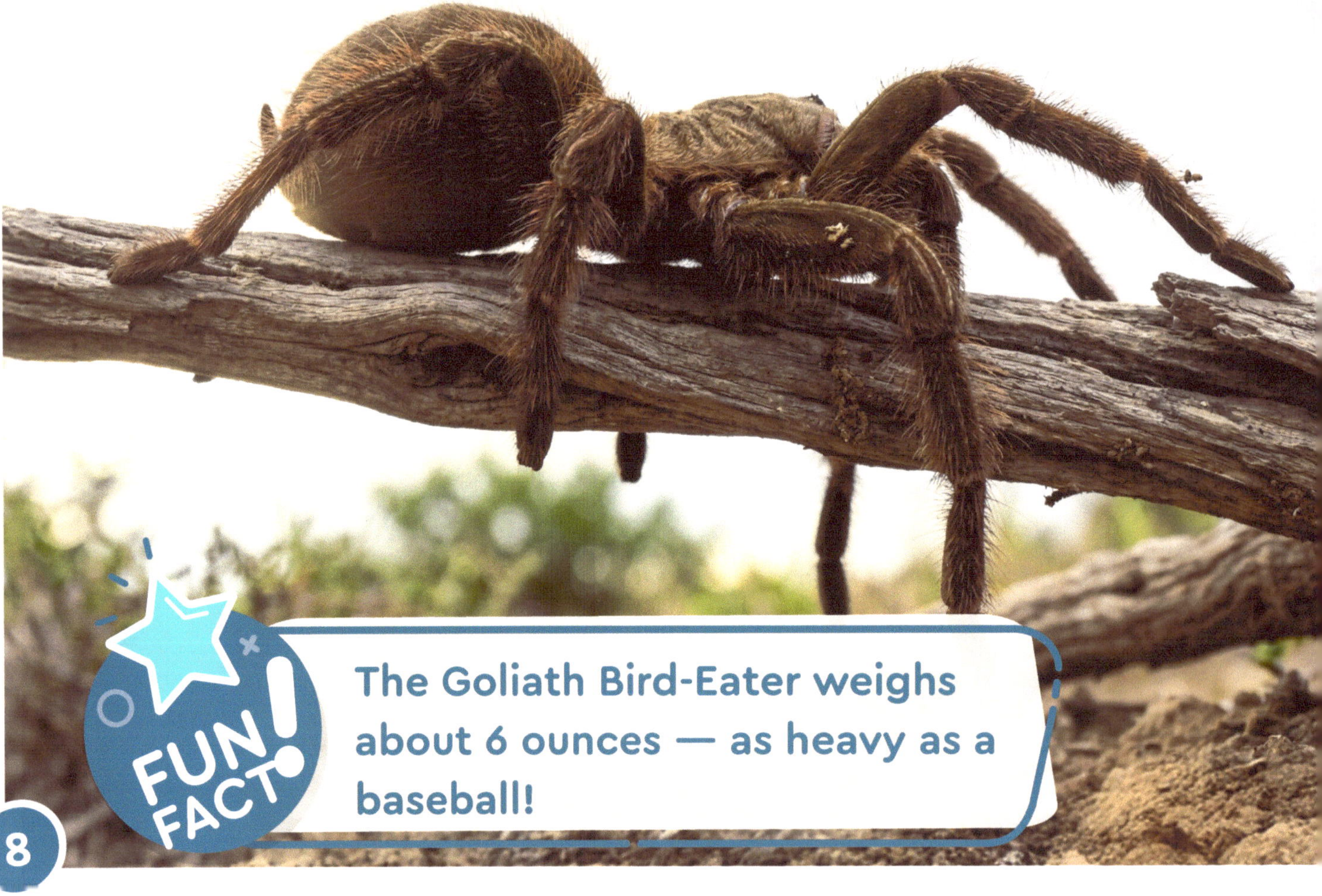

FUN FACT!

The Goliath Bird-Eater weighs about 6 ounces — as heavy as a baseball!

Thump! A huge tarantula stretches its legs wide on a log.

Tarantulas come in many sizes. Some are as small as a grape. Others are as big as a dinner plate!

The Goliath Bird-Eater is the biggest spider in the world. Its legs can spread nearly 12 inches across. That is about as wide as a classroom ruler!

Most tarantulas fit in the palm of your hand. Even a small one looks big and bold. Those thick legs and round, fuzzy bodies fool your eyes into thinking they are even larger.

HAIRY HUNTERS

Click! A tarantula's eight legs tap across the fallen log.

A tarantula's body has two main parts. The front part holds the eyes, mouth, and fangs. The back part makes silk.

Eight long legs help the spider walk and climb. Each leg is covered with tiny hairs. Two short feelers near the mouth help it taste and touch the world around it.

The Greenbottle Blue has bright blue legs and a shiny green body. It is one of the most colorful spiders on Earth. Even its hairs shine in the light!

FEEL FIRST

FUN FACT!

Some tarantulas can smell using special hairs on their feet — they taste the ground as they walk!

Buzz! A Cobalt Blue tarantula feels the hum of a beetle through the soil.

Tarantulas do not see well at all. They have eight tiny eyes, but they can only see light and dark. Touch is their best sense by far.

The tiny hairs on their legs pick up small shakes in the ground. When a bug walks near, the spider feels it. The hairs also sense wind and heat.

The Cobalt Blue waits deep in its burrow. It feels the ground shake when prey gets close. Then it strikes in a flash!

FLING FUZZ

Tarantulas grow back the hairs they flick — a fresh coat appears after each molt!

Flick! A tarantula kicks a cloud of tiny hairs at a hungry bird.

Some tarantulas have a clever trick. When scared, they kick tiny hairs off their belly. These hairs float in the air and sting!

The hairs bother the eyes and nose of attackers. They are so small you can barely see them. But they make predators back away fast.

The Mexican Red Knee is great at this defense. It flicks hairs to scare off foxes and birds. A bald patch on its belly shows where the hairs came off.

BUG BUFFET

A tarantula can go a whole month without eating — then gobble down a huge meal in one night!

Crunch! A tarantula munches on a big, juicy cricket.

Tarantulas eat bugs and other small animals. Crickets, beetles, and grasshoppers are some of their top meals. They even eat worms and small lizards.

These spiders do not chew their food. They squirt juice onto prey to make it soft. Then they slurp it all up like soup!

The Goliath Bird-Eater eats more than bugs. It can catch frogs, mice, and even small snakes. Someone once saw one eating a bird — that is how it got its famous name!

AMBUSH ATTACK

FUN FACT!

Tarantula venom works fast — prey stops moving within 30 seconds of a bite!

Snap! A tarantula lunges at a passing beetle with lightning speed.

Tarantulas do not chase their food. They sit and wait near the opening of their burrow. When something gets close, they pounce!

Speed is the key. A tarantula waits for a bug to walk by, then grabs the prey with its front legs. A quick bite with its fangs ends the hunt in seconds.

The King Baboon is a fierce hunter. It hides just inside its burrow and listens. When a cricket steps too close, it rushes out. In a blink, the cricket is caught!

WATCH OUT

DID YOU KNOW?
The tarantula hawk wasp can grow 2 inches long — and has one of the most painful stings on Earth!

Screech! A tarantula freezes as a hungry hawk swoops down low.

Even big spiders have enemies. Birds, lizards, and snakes all eat tarantulas.

The Pink Toe tarantula lives in trees in South America. Up high, it must watch out for birds and bats. Staying still and hiding is its best plan for survival.

Some wasps hunt them, too. The tarantula hawk wasp is a scary enemy. It stings a tarantula to freeze its body. Then it lays an egg on the spider. The baby wasp eats the spider as it grows. Creepy!

STAY SAFE

Some tarantulas can swim short distances — they trap air in their body hairs to float!

Whoosh! A tarantula darts back into its silk-lined burrow to hide.

Tarantulas have many ways to stay safe. Running away is often the first choice. A quick dash into a burrow keeps them out of sight.

Some tarantulas rear up on their back legs to look big and scary. Others make hissing sounds by rubbing their legs together. These tricks can scare off predators.

The Greenbottle Blue spins webs all around its home. The webs act like a fence. If the silk moves, the spider knows danger is near and can prepare to fight or flee.

EIGHT LEGS
DID YOU KNOW?
A tarantula can pump liquid into its legs to stretch them out — like tiny water balloons!
24

Tap, tap, tap! A tarantula walks on eight legs up a tall tree.

Tarantulas walk with all eight legs at once. Four legs move on one side, then four move on the other. This gives them a smooth, steady walk.

Some tarantulas are fast runners. They can sprint in short bursts to catch prey or escape danger. But they get tired quickly and must rest.

The Pink Toe tarantula is a great climber. It has tiny claws and silk pads on its feet that help it grip bark tight. It can even walk upside down on branches!

NIGHT LIFE

After a big meal, a tarantula may rest in its burrow for a full week without moving!

26

Shuffle! A tarantula pushes out of its burrow as the sky turns dark.

Tarantulas are nocturnal. That means they are active at night. During the day, they rest in their burrows or hiding spots.

When darkness falls, they come out to hunt and explore. The cool night air keeps them from getting too hot. They may spend hours creeping along the ground looking for food.

The Cobalt Blue tarantula is very shy. It spends most of its time deep inside its burrow. It only comes out when it is dark and quiet outside.

LONER LIFE

Scurry! A tarantula looks out its burrow, no friends in sight.

Tarantulas like to be alone. They do not live in groups or packs. Each spider has its own burrow and its own space.

If two tarantulas meet, they may fight. They do not share food or shelter. A lone tarantula is a happy tarantula!

The King Baboon is known for its bad temper. It does not want any animal near its home. If one gets too close, it will strike fast and hard.

A few rare tarantulas in South America actually share burrows — scientists call them "social spiders"!

DARING DANCE

Male tarantulas only live 3 to 7 years, but females can live 30 years or more!

Drum, drum! A male tarantula taps his legs to call for a mate.

Mating is risky for a male tarantula. He must find a female and not get eaten! Males wander far from home to look for a mate.

When he finds one, he does a dance. He taps the ground and waves his legs. If the female likes him, she lets him close. If not, he runs for his life!

The Mexican Red Knee male may walk for miles searching. After they mate, he must leave fast. If he stays too long the hungry female may try to eat him!

TINY TOTS

DID YOU KNOW
Baby tarantulas shed their skin for the first time within just one week of hatching!

Crack! Hundreds of tiny tarantulas wiggle free from their egg sacs.

A mother tarantula lays her eggs in a silk sac. She may lay 50 to 2,000 eggs at once! The tiny eggs sit snug inside the sac for weeks.

When the babies hatch, they are called spiderlings. At first, they are pale and very small. They stay close to the egg sac until they grow stronger.

Pink Toe spiderlings are bright blue when they hatch! As they grow, their color slowly changes. They turn the pink and brown of their parents over time.

MOM DUTY

DID YOU KNOW?

If the eggs do not hatch, some mother tarantulas eat the whole egg sac for energy!

Patter! A mother tarantula gently rolls her egg sac back and forth.

Mother tarantulas guard their egg sacs day and night. They do not let any animal come near. Some carry the sac with them wherever they go.

The mother turns the egg sac often to keep all the eggs warm. She does not eat while she guards them. All her time goes to keeping them safe.

A Goliath Bird-Eater mother is a fierce guard. She wraps her huge body around the egg sac. No predator dares come close to this giant spider!

SUPER SURVIVORS

A molting tarantula flips completely onto its back and lies still for hours — it looks dead, but it is just waiting for its new skin to form!

Pop! A tarantula sheds its old skin and comes out looking brand new.

Tarantulas are remarkable survivors, and one of their most surprising tricks is molting. As a tarantula grows, it sheds its entire skin in one piece — legs, fangs, and all.

If a tarantula loses a leg to a predator, it can grow it back during the next molt. A brand new leg, fully functional, right where the old one was!

The Cobalt Blue tarantula of Southeast Asia takes survival even further. It spends most of its life deep inside a burrow, perfectly hidden from heat, cold, and anything that might want to eat it.

SPOT ONE!

FUN
FACT!
There are over 900 different kinds of tarantulas — and scientists discover new ones every year!

Crackle! Dry leaves shift as a tarantula moves across the trail.

You can spot tarantulas in the wild without traveling far. In the United States, the best places to look are the deserts and grasslands of the Southwest — Texas, Arizona, New Mexico, and California are all home to several species.

Go out at dusk with a flashlight when tarantulas are most active. Move slowly and look near rocks, logs, and small burrow holes in the ground. Males often wander in the open during fall, searching for a mate.

If you spot one, stay still and enjoy the view from a safe distance. Never touch a wild tarantula — just look and observe!

GLOSSARY

burrow

A hole or tunnel an animal digs in the ground

venom

A poison that some animals use to stun or kill prey

dusk

The time of day just after the sun sets

molt

When an animal sheds its old skin to grow a new one

nocturnal

Active at night and resting during the day